SEASONS OF PRAYER

SEASONS *of* PRAYER

Resources for Worship

LISA WITHROW

First published 1995 in Great Britain
The Society for Promoting Christian Knowledge
Holy Trinity Church
Marylebone Road
London
NW1 4DU

British Library Cataloguing in Publication Data

A catalogue record for this book is available from the British Library.

ISBN 0-281-04828-2

These services were compiled by Lisa Withrow, a Minister of the United Methodist
Church, when serving in a Church of Scotland parish. They are published for use in
churches of any denomination in circumstances in which the minister has discretion
to decide the order of service.
They are not official or authorized liturgies of the Church of England, the Church of
Scotland, or any other Christian body.

Typeset by Pioneer Associates Ltd., Perthshire

Printed in Great Britain at
The University Press, Cambridge

CONTENTS

Contents

Contents

ACKNOWLEDGEMENTS

I am deeply grateful to the congregation of Jordanhill Parish Church, Glasgow, whose experiences of life and faith provided the environment in which to worship with many of the liturgical resources presented here. The material in *Seasons of Prayer* comes out of a community's journey with God that was and is dynamic, sometimes surprising, and never complete; many of the people at Jordanhill were eager to encounter God's word in new ways as they travelled this journey of faith. Thus, they were open to alternative language and creative liturgy—they were in large part co-creators of this resource book.

Thanks are due to Finlay Macdonald who wrote and contributed the previously unpublished eucharistic poem and summer canticle found in this volume in adapted form.

I would also like to express my gratitude to Gretchen Wetherill, a laywoman in the United Methodist tradition, for reading this text and making suggestions and corrections in the light of her own creative contribution to the world of liturgical drama.

PREFACE

As we grow older, we understand our relationships differently. Our parents are not the same people in our minds now as they were when we were small children. Our friendships have changed in focus and quality since we were young. Our concepts of living and loving vary too as we grow through different life-experiences. Likewise, our encounters and conversations with God take on new dimensions as our faith journey matures.

Worship is the primary response Christians make to God's presence among us, by focusing on the divine-human relationship. Gathering together for ritual and liturgy, song and silence, and metaphor and movement in worship gives us the space to speak and listen in God's name while building relationships with each other.

Often in the ministry I have heard comments from people which sound something like this: 'I keep searching for a deeper relationship with God, yet I do not seem to be able to find what I am looking for.' I have also heard the quiet longing in their voices. They are searching deeply like the psalmist in Psalm 42.1–2 (NRSV): 'As a deer longs for flowing streams, so my soul longs for you, O God. My soul thirsts for God, for the living God.'

Part of the search that I am convinced every active soul undergoes at one time or another involves looking for alternative ways of communicating with God. In worship there is room to examine our relationship with our Creator in terms of how we 'see' and hear God's presence and how we speak with God. As faith journeys mature, new possibilities open. As dialogue with God becomes more important in building relationships between human beings and God, words and images speak more loudly. While some people wish to retain the tradition in which they have grown up, others search for more intimate and more inclusive styles of liturgy.

The volume of resources offered here attempts to strike a balance between traditional worship style and more personal, inclusive possibilities. It is an offering of hope for those who search for alternative ways to worship, while at the same time remaining simply an

1

initial step in the journey to expand the Christian church's use of liturgical metaphor and image. The resources are also reminders of the history which has brought our worship to its current day. As the prayers, liturgies and readings speak to us through the seasons of the liturgical year—the ancient rhythms of the church—they call us to remember the sacredness of our relationship with God while we move through the cycle of our own lives.

The materials before you have developed over time in an active church community in Scotland, where a number of people, by quietly asking for something more than what traditional liturgies were offering them, called forth these prayers and readings. Most of the resources here have been tried, re-worked and polished for a number of years both in and outside Scotland. However, I invite worship leaders in other places, times and settings to use these writings freely, as a spring-board for your own writing. The material lends itself to adaptation to your own environment, sense of the human condition, and ecclesiastical concerns. Likewise, this volume can easily be used as a supplement to resources which worship leaders may already have.

By sharing a combination of well-accepted words and images with language and imagery that may seem born of a different genre—without being radically unprecedented in a given church setting—we connect the old with the new, the past with the present, and tradition with possibility. Through worship in this way, a new door is opened to our intellect, senses, imagination, experience and our very souls, connecting us in unique ways with the movements of God. For those who search, for those who yearn, may these words become a creative way of belonging in a place called the Christian community.

Part One

THE GREAT THANKSGIVINGS

Eucharistic Prayers

INTRODUCTION

The Eucharist or Holy Communion gathers together people of faith to eat bread and drink wine in remembrance of the last supper, as Christ commanded. While remembering God's acts on earth and Christ's saving death on the cross, we in turn offer ourselves to God through this holy meal.

The eucharistic/communion prayers contain several elements: gratitude to God, reminders of God's acts for humanity, an offering of ourselves to God, a blessing upon the bread and wine and an invitation to eat in Christ's name. The language focuses on eating the meal together as an act of remembrance and thanksgiving for Christ's presence and sacrifice for us, rather than on participating in a solemn occasion where the 'unworthy' are not particularly welcome. Indeed, the Greek *eucharistia* translates as 'thanksgiving'. Christ has made us all welcome to his table as a people who wish to know his forgiveness and feel his grace. May we celebrate together!

Possibilities for worship

These seasonal prayers were originally used in a Scottish reformed setting; subsequently, they have been adapted and used internationally in various ecumenical worship services. Over the years, each eucharistic/communion prayer has been spoken in a creative manner or within a creatively decorated space. The prayers are each accompanied by individual ideas for worship and added symbolism, along with suggestions for the use of several voices. The worship leader may try these ideas or adapt them as appropriate.

ADVENT

May God be with you
and also with you.
Lift up your hearts.
We lift them up to Christ.
Let us give thanks to our Redeemer.
It is right to give our thanks and praise.

We praise you, Eternal Loving God.
You made the ages a preparation for the coming of a Saviour.
In this age and season, we wait again with expectant hearts
and hopeful spirits,
yearning for your presence among us.
We hear the apostle's word:
'Rejoice in the Lord always! The Lord is at hand!'
So we join our celebration to the adoration of all your people in
heaven and earth, singing (saying):

Holy, holy, holy one, God of power and might;
heaven and earth are full of your glory.
Glory be to you, O God most high.
Blessed is one who comes in the name of the Saviour.
Hosanna in the highest!

Powerful God,
the one in whom our mothers and fathers trusted and were not
disappointed,
we praise your holy name.

God of Sarah and Abraham,
God of Moses and Miriam,
God of Deborah and Gideon,

God of Joseph and Mary,
God of countless generations,
of men and women unknown to us
but known and loved by you,
we give thanks to you for bringing us salvation in the coming of
the Messiah.

Long ago, the Redeemer came in the humble birth of a child,
a child of your amazing and divine love,
a child of Mary's 'yes' to you,
a child of Joseph's acceptance,
the child of our salvation.

Long ago, the Saviour took the bread and broke it,
gave thanks to you,
gave it to his disciples and said:
'Take, eat. This is my body broken for you.
Do this in remembrance of me.'
And he took the cup,
gave thanks to you,
shared it with his disciples and said:
'Drink from it, all of you.
This is my blood shed for you for the forgiveness of sins.
Do this in remembrance of me.'

And now we find the presence of our Saviour through these
symbols of his body and blood,
signs of your word made flesh.
Pour out your Spirit upon us, God of grace and God of glory;
bless this bread and wine,
hallow this gathering of your community of faith,
make our hearts into a cradle for our Saviour.
As you give Christ to and for us,
so we give ourselves for him,
in obedience to his call
and in devotion to his name.

THE LORD'S PRAYER

BREAKING THE BREAD AND SHARING THE WINE
Take, eat. This is the body of Christ given for you and for me.
Do this in remembrance of him.
Take, drink. This cup is the new covenant in the blood of Christ.
Drink from it and remember him.

THE INVITATION
Draw near to the holy table in faith and in love.

PRAYER (*following the meal*)
God of promise, we thank you for your gifts of bread and wine.
Make them be for us sources of love and strength during this
time of expectation.
Through the promise of Christ's coming, fortify us to be your
servants in the world.
All honour and glory are yours, Lover of Souls. **Amen.**

Ideas for worship

*This Advent prayer may be used both in a formal worship setting and in
a small group. In the smaller setting (chancel or chapel area, or a room
arranged for worship), the list of saints may be read by female and male
voices from different parts of the room. Advent candles may be used to
symbolize the marking of time before the Christ-child's birth. The worship
leader may wish to light additional candles during intervals in the
eucharistic prayer to create pinpoints of light during a dark time of year;
these candles symbolize the light of Christ coming into a troubled world.*

CHRISTMAS

May God be with you
and also with you.
Lift up your hearts.
We lift them up to Christ.
Let us give thanks to our Redeemer.
It is right to give our thanks and praise.

Glorious God, it is right indeed to give thanks and praise to your
name.
At the birth of our Saviour, shepherds lifted their eyes to a vision
of angels.
Eastern star-watchers saw a sign in the heavens.
Two people raised their faces in praise for a child born in a stable.
So now we lift our own eyes, our hearts and voices, in praise of
your name.
We join with the angels and archangels in the ancient hymn of
praise, singing (saying):

Holy, holy, holy one, God of power and might;
heaven and earth are full of your glory.
Glory be to you, O God most high.
Blessed is one who comes in the name of the Saviour,
Hosanna in the highest!

All-seeing God, with gratitude and love we remember your mighty
acts.
In the beginning your Word created heaven and earth,
called forth a people to be your people,
proclaimed and prophesied your message of hope and salvation,
and in the fullness of time,
was made flesh in Christ Jesus.
We praise you, O God, for your Word.

All-loving God, as a father cares for his children,
as a mother leads her young,
you brought your people out of bondage in Egypt
to a land flowing with milk and honey;
and in the fullness of time,
you yourself became a child in Jesus Christ,
nourished and guided by his parents in their home.
We praise you, O God, for your love.

Today, with gratitude,
we remember Christ's birth,
his teaching,
his healing,
his suffering,
his death,
his resurrection and ascension.
At the celebration of Christ's birth,
we also remember the night in which he was betrayed;
he took bread
and when he had blessed it and given thanks,
he broke it and said:
'Take, eat. This is my body which is broken for you.
Do this in remembrance of me.'
After the supper, he took the cup and said:
'This is the new covenant in my blood.
Do this, as often as you drink it, in remembrance of me.'

As we remember all your mighty acts, O God of mystery,
send your Holy Spirit upon us and upon this bread and wine,
that by your sanctifying grace our hearts may be made holy
and our lives may be made pure.
We offer our own lives to you in praise and thanksgiving
at this celebration of Christ's birth.
May this feast become for us a true communion with one another
and with Christ our Saviour.

THE LORD'S PRAYER

BREAKING THE BREAD AND SHARING THE WINE
Take, eat. This is the body of Christ broken for us all.
Do this in remembrance of him.
Take, drink. This is the cup of the new covenant.
Drink from it in remembrance of him.

THE INVITATION
Draw near to the table set before you in faith and in love.

PRAYER *(following the meal)*
Gracious God, you have given us the gift of Jesus Christ.
As we have remembered your mighty acts in this meal together,
we remember too that we are called to be your servants in the world.
Bless us as we welcome the Light of the World in praise and
thanksgiving! **Amen.**

Ideas for worship

*This Christmas prayer may be used in both early and late-night
Christmas Eve services as well as on Christmas Day. On Christmas Eve,
when the sanctuary lighting is dimmed, special lighting may be used to
enhance both the Advent wreath with the Christ-candle and the eucharistic elements. Male and female clergy may read alternate paragraphs in
the prayer. A worship leader may choose to use sung settings of the
Sanctus within the prayer. People may be invited to come forward to a
place near the Advent wreath to receive the elements, and then take a
small candle lit from the Christ-candle back to their seats, symbolizing
the light of Christ in their own lives.*

EPIPHANY

May God be with you
and also with you.
Lift up your hearts.
We lift them up to Christ.
Let us give thanks to our Redeemer.
It is right to give our thanks and praise.

It is right and good to give praise to your name, Almighty God.
You will us into being,
you love us into faith,
you inspire us to live out our calling as followers of Jesus Christ.
Creating, Redeeming and Sustaining God, we praise your name
and join the heavenly host together with your people here on earth
singing (saying):

Holy, holy, holy one, God of power and might;
heaven and earth are full of your glory.
Glory be to you, O God most high.
Blessed is one who comes in the name of the Saviour,
Hosanna in the highest!

God of wisdom, with gratitude and love we remember your mighty
acts.
You created a world that was good.
You gave us this earth to enjoy.
You trusted us to share with you in caring for it.
And when we sinned,
you still did not abandon us,
but made covenant with our ancestors.
You called your people to yourself,
led them from slavery to freedom,

gave them the law to obey,
prophetic teaching to follow,
and songs of hope to sing.

Then, God of unending grace,
you sent your Son, Christ Jesus,
born of a woman,
to be the glory of your people Israel,
a light to shine in the darkness.
To this light came travellers from the east,
those already wise seeking higher wisdom.
Finding greater wisdom in a young child than they had ever
known,
they offered their precious gifts.
This child of Mary and Joseph was indeed the Son of God,
the one who revealed your glory,
transforming sin to goodness,
disease to health,
despair to hope,
sorrow to joy,
and death to life.

Yet he, too, knew sorrow and death,
bearing upon himself the sin of the world at Calvary:
betrayed, deserted, crucified.
And on the night in which he was betrayed,
he took bread,
blessed it,
gave thanks and broke it,
shared it with his companions and said:
'This is my body broken for you.
Take, eat, do this in remembrance of me.'
In the same manner, he took the cup, blessed it and said:
'Drink from this, all of you.
This cup is the new covenant in my blood;
do this, as often as you drink it, in remembrance of me.'

God of wisdom and light, send your Holy Spirit upon us
and upon this bread and wine.
As we come together to eat at your table,
we offer ourselves to you in praise and thanksgiving for your
mighty acts.

THE LORD'S PRAYER

BREAKING THE BREAD AND SHARING THE WINE
Take, eat. This is the body of Christ broken for you.
Do this in remembrance of him.
Take, drink. This is the blood of Christ shed for you.
Do this in remembrance of him.

THE INVITATION
Draw near to the table of sustenance and love.

PRAYER (*following the meal*)
Giver of Life, let your light shine upon us.
May your grace be in our midst.
May your wisdom be our guide.
Here, may the meeting of Christ with each one
strengthen our faith,
enrich our witness,
and bring us closer to the Light of Christ,
now and forevermore. **Amen**.

Ideas for worship

The Epiphany prayer may be accompanied by various settings of the
Sanctus *used for a congregational sung response. Musical settings can be
found in most hymnals or supplementary musical resources. The eucharis-
tic/communion meal may follow a dialogue sermon involving the meeting
of the Magi and the holy family in Bethlehem. The prayer itself may be
spoken in several voices.*

LENT

May God be with you
and also with you.
Lift up your hearts.
We lift them up to Christ.
Let us give thanks to our Redeemer.
It is right to give our thanks and praise.

We give our thanks and praise to the God who leads us on our
journeys;
you accompany us to the cross and steady us when we stumble,
strengthen us when we wish to hide.
You call us to follow you while you shoulder our burdens.
You forgive our sins.
In the forty days of Lent,
we remember the love you made manifest
in the birth, life and death of Christ.

In Christ's healing acts and radical teachings
as he walked toward his own death,
we recall the words that he spoke
to call forth love, care and respect for one another.
We are grateful for your assurance of love amidst human betrayal,
care amidst hatred,
and respect amidst oppression.
Therefore, we join together in singing (saying):

Holy, holy, holy one, God of power and might;
heaven and earth are full of your glory.
Glory be to you, O God most high.
Blessed is one who comes in the name of the Saviour.
Hosanna in the highest!

We turn our hearts to you in this season of repentance and cleansing.
As Jesus took time to be with you before he was taken to his trial and death,
we take time now to humble ourselves before you in the hope of finding your transforming grace.

(*Silent prayer*)

We remember the last time Jesus and his disciples ate together at table;
he broke the bread and shared the cup,
blessing them and saying to his companions:
'Do this in remembrance of me.'
So, today, we break the bread, we share the cup,
and we remember the mercy and love of Jesus Christ.

In gratitude for Christ's sacrifice for our sake,
we offer ourselves to you.
We partake now in the meal which brings us together as disciples,
and sends us forth as renewed people.
Bless these elements, we pray.

THE LORD'S PRAYER

BREAKING THE BREAD AND SHARING THE WINE
Take, eat. This is the body of Christ given for all.
Do this in remembrance of him.
This cup is the new covenant in the blood of Christ.
Drink from it and remember him.

THE INVITATION
Draw near to the holy table as a forgiven and redeemed people.

PRAYER (*following the meal*)
Redeemer of life, bless this table-gathering of your people.
May the sacrifice that Christ chose for us make us thankful.
May the supper that Christ shared with us today strengthen us in
our witness to the world.
In our Saviour's name. **Amen.**

Ideas for worship

*The Lenten prayer is shorter and quieter than other seasonal eucharistic
prayers. It contains undertones of confession throughout the thanksgiving
in keeping with the Lenten season. This prayer has been used in formal
worship at times, but more often in small-group settings in a side-chancel
or chapel. The tone of the worship is corporately confessional. Slowness
of reading, punctuated by silence, emphasizes the focus on reflection and
humility appropriate for the season. One candle may be lit at the side of
the elements to symbolize Christ's presence with us; in general, it is appropriate to have dim lighting.*

PALM SUNDAY

May God be with you
and also with you.
Lift up your hearts.
We lift them up to Christ.
Let us give thanks to our Redeemer.
It is right to give our thanks and praise.

It is good to praise your name, Creator God, liberator of lives.
All generations proclaim your goodness,
and today the whole company of saints in heaven and on earth are
praising you and singing (saying):

Holy, holy, holy one, God of power and might;
heaven and earth are full of your glory.
Hosanna in the highest!
Blessed is one who comes in the name of the Saviour.
Hosanna in the highest!

We recall today, Sovereign God,
how your Son entered the city of Jerusalem.
He came humbly, mounted on a colt
and was welcomed with loud hosannas.
Yet the joyful acclamation was soon to turn to angry condemnation;
joyous, loud hosannas soon became cruel cries of 'crucify'.
Indeed, the one who would have gathered the children of Jerusalem
as a hen gathers her chicks under her wing,
was mocked,
derided,
rejected.
Yet through it all, Christ showed
strength through his gentleness,

wisdom in his quietness,
depth of meaning in his silence.

Sustaining God, you were with your Son at his death,
you raised him on the third day
and redeemed us all.
Today, we celebrate your presence in Christ
and with us all
as we walk through the valley of the shadow of death
into new life.
Help us now to open our hearts to him
that he may enter into them
as he entered Jerusalem on that Palm Sunday.
Help us to offer the hosannas of our lips and the homage of our
hearts,
serving him in loyalty and love all our days.

As he shared bread and wine with his disciples during their last
meal together,
he blessed grain and grape,
gave thanks to you and said:
'Eat and drink these in remembrance of me.'
And now again, send your Holy Spirit upon us,
and upon these gifts of bread and wine.
May these ordinary elements become the channels of holiness and
grace
by which our souls are fed;
may we know the gifts of truth, joy and peace
as we offer ourselves to you in praise and thanksgiving.

THE LORD'S PRAYER

BREAKING THE BREAD AND SHARING THE WINE
Take, eat. This is the body of Christ given for you.
Take, drink from the cup of the new covenant.
Do these things in remembrance of him.

THE INVITATION
Draw near to this table of redeeming love.

PRAYER (*following the meal*)
Redeeming One, may these elements strengthen us for the journey.
Through bread and wine, may we be sanctified by Christ for
service in our world;
May the Saviour's peace and grace be with us as we follow him in
faith. **Amen**.

Ideas for worship

*Palm Sunday lends itself both to an acknowledgement and celebration of
Jesus as the Christ and to a foreboding sense of betrayal and death to come.
Liturgical drama may prove effective, where one or two biblical person-
alities involved in the events leading to the crucifixion and burial are
portrayed. Moving worship can be developed by dramatically reading and
interpreting the triumphal entry into Jerusalem, followed by prayers of
thanksgiving and anthems. Then, dramatic reading may help to move the
congregation into the realm of events up to and including the last supper.
The culmination of the worship takes place in the eucharistic/communion
prayer and meal together. Grey cloth can replace the liturgical purple or
white colours after the meal.*

MAUNDY THURSDAY

May God be with you
and also with you.
Lift up your hearts.
We lift them up to Christ.
Let us give thanks to our Redeemer.
It is right to give our thanks and praise.

Tonight, we give you thanks and praise.
Loving God, we remember your love in the presence of Jesus
Christ.
Living God, we remember your love made manifest, and Christ's
life laid down on the cross.
Tonight, we remember Jesus sharing a last supper with his
companions;
laying aside his garments,
taking a towel,
pouring water,
washing feet.
We remember Jesus taking and breaking bread,
blessing and sharing the cup and saying:
'Do this in remembrance of me.'
So tonight, we break the bread, we share the cup
and we remember Jesus Christ in gratitude and love.

We praise your name, Holy One.
Your grace still permeates our world,
turning despair to hope
and pain to peace,
if only we were more responsive to it.
Tonight we remember the holiness which emptied itself,
poured itself out in the bitter betrayal and abandonment at
Gethsemane,

saying as the disciples slept,
'Not my will, but yours be done.'

In humble gratitude for the greatest act of love through your Son,
we give you thanks that you became vulnerable for our sake.
Therefore, we praise you with all your people, saying:

Holy, holy, holy one, God of power and might;
heaven and earth are full of your glory.
Glory be to you, O God most high.
Blessed is one who comes in the name of the Saviour,
Hosanna in the highest.

Come upon us now, in the power of the Holy Spirit;
and as Christ blessed the bread and the wine in the upper room,
so bless us as we gather in this place.
May we sit at the table with our Saviour,
share in the feast of his self-giving love,
offer ourselves to him,
faithfully serve him in the world
and look forward to the fullness of his eternal reign.

THE LORD'S PRAYER

At the last supper, Jesus took the bread,
gave thanks, broke the bread and said:
'This is my body, broken for you.
Do this in remembrance of me.'
At the last supper, Jesus took the cup,
gave thanks, shared the cup and said:
'This cup is the new covenant in my blood.
Do this as often as you drink it, in remembrance of me.'

Lamb of God, you take away the sins of the world.
Have mercy on us.
Lamb of God, you take away the sins of the world.
Have mercy on us.
Lamb of God, you take away the sins of the world.
Grant us your peace.

BREAKING THE BREAD AND SHARING THE WINE
Take, eat, this is Christ's body, given for you.
Take, drink, this is Christ's blood, shed for you.

THE INVITATION
Draw near to the table in remembrance of him.

PRAYER (*following the meal*)
Sustainer and Redeemer, we give you thanks in our sharing of
bread and wine.
On this night of betrayal, may we remain faithful.
May these elements keep us strong as we journey with Christ to
the cross. **Amen.**

Ideas for worship

The Maundy Thursday prayer reads simply. The tone is quiet, for in addition to thanksgiving, there is a sense of a momentous event taking place—betrayal of Christ. In the past, each time this prayer has been used in any worship setting, it has been followed immediately by a scripture reading and hymn describing the disciples going with Jesus to the Garden of Gethsemane. After singing, a number of designated people remove the elements from the communion table/altar and others remove all symbolism, decoration and colour from the chancel. The congregation departs in silence.

EASTER

May God be with you
and also with you.
Lift up your hearts.
We lift them up to Christ.
Let us give thanks to our Redeemer.
It is right to give our thanks and praise.

We remember Jesus in the garden appearing to Mary and calling
her by name.
Come, risen Christ!
Come, risen Christ!
Help us to remember that you know us each intimately and that
you call us by name.
(*Pause*)

We remember Jesus appearing to the disciples and saying, 'Peace
be with you.'
Come, risen Christ!
Come, risen Christ!
Grant us your peace.
(*Pause*)

We remember Jesus appearing to Thomas and saying, 'Do not
doubt, but believe.'
Come, risen Christ!
Come, risen Christ!
Help us to rise above our doubts and fears and to trust completely
in your name.
(*Pause*)

We remember Jesus walking on the road to Emmaus, talking with his followers.
Come, risen Christ!
Come, risen Christ!
Open to us the Scripture and help us to know your truth.
(*Pause*)

We remember Jesus sharing breakfast on the beach with his companions.
Come, risen Christ!
Come, risen Christ!
Be to us the bread of life.
(*Pause*)

We remember Jesus commanding his disciples to tell the good news to all people and to baptize in his name.
Come, risen Christ!
Come, risen Christ!
Help us to be your witnesses in the world. Hear us as we praise your name together:

Holy, holy, holy one, God of power and might;
heaven and earth are full of your glory.
Hosanna in the highest!
Blessed is one who comes in the name of the Saviour,
Hosanna in the highest!

We remember Christ sharing bread and wine with his disciples on the night of Judas' betrayal.
Today, we share bread and wine in remembrance of his death and resurrection.
We pray, O God of new life, that you will pour out your Holy Spirit here upon us and upon these elements,
making them be for us the new covenant in Christ.
Bless them and us as we offer ourselves to you in thanksgiving for

your sacrifice on our behalf.
All praise and glory to you, O God!

THE LORD'S PRAYER

BREAKING THE BREAD AND SHARING THE WINE
Jesus said at the last supper:
'Take, eat. This is my body given for you.
Do this in remembrance of me.
This cup is the new covenant in my blood.
Drink from it, all of you, and remember me.'

THE INVITATION
Draw near to the table together, rejoicing in the resurrection of
our Saviour.

PRAYER (*following the meal*)
God of new life, you have given us hope through the resurrection
of our Saviour.
Through the breaking of bread and sharing of wine, we come to
know new life in you.
Bless this meal which we have shared.
Send us forth to sing songs of thanksgiving in your name! **Amen**.

Ideas for worship

The Easter service is triumphant and this prayer is written in a celebra-
tory tone. It may be prayed with more than one voice and can be adapt-
ed to three or more voices. The prayer is written here in a responsive style.
A white lily placed before the communion table/altar helps to symbolize
the resurrection celebration, and having the elements and the lily brought
forward during a triumphant hymn also adds movement and a sense of
change-over from the Lenten season.

27

ASCENSION

May God be with you
and also with you.
Lift up your hearts.
We lift them up to Christ.
Let us give thanks to our Redeemer.
It is right to give our thanks and praise.

Amazing One,
we give you thanks and praise for your acts upon all the earth,
glorifying you in your grace and righteousness for our sake.
Hear our hymn of thanksgiving as we lift our voices to heaven,
praising your name and singing (saying):

Holy, holy, holy one, God of power and might;
heaven and earth are full of your glory.
Glory be to you, O God most high.
Blessed is one who comes in the name of the Saviour,
Hosanna in the highest!

God of miracles, God of power,
you have accompanied us through time,
and in that journey of centuries
you saw fit to give us the gift of your Son, Jesus Christ.
You called us to follow him, your beloved Son,
and then promised through him
that you would continue with us along the way,
with the power of the Holy Spirit.

We praise you for Christ's coming to us.
We praise you for Christ's returning to you
in the glory of a dazzling cloud

to the amazement of all disciples.
We praise you for the assurance of your Counsellor and
Comforter
coming to the disciples
and remaining with all your followers until the end of time.

On this day, as we celebrate the ascension of our Saviour,
we ask for your presence here in our meal of thanksgiving;
in our celebration, we also remember the night when Jesus gave
himself up for us,
when he sat at table with his disciples,
breaking bread and drinking wine with them.
And as they shared, Jesus took the loaf, broke it,
gave it to the disciples and said:
'Take and eat. This is my body broken for you.
Do this and remember me.'
Then he took the cup, blessed it and said:
'Drink from this, all of you.
This is the new covenant in my blood.
Do this and remember me.'

So we eat and drink in remembrance of Christ our Saviour,
risen and ascended in glory.
God Eternal, we ask your presence here with us
and your blessing on this bread and wine.
May we offer ourselves to you in the sharing of this meal
that we may be disciples called to go forth in your name.
Great Provider, we give praise and thanks to you forevermore.

THE LORD'S PRAYER

BREAKING THE BREAD AND SHARING THE WINE
Take, eat. This is the body of Christ broken for you.
Do this in remembrance of him.
Take, drink. This is the blood of Christ shed for you.
Do this in remembrance of him.

THE INVITATION
Draw near to these gifts and partake in the goodness of our
Saviour.

PRAYER (*following the meal*)
Glorious Light, Generous Love,
we give you thanks for this meal shared in your name.
May it be sustenance for us, your disciples in the world.
May it be a reminder to us of all your mighty acts for us.
May it be a continued blessing to us through the coming of the
Mighty Counsellor, now and forevermore. **Amen.**

Ideas for worship

*Particularly striking on Ascension Day is the elevating of the elements
when speaking the words of blessing and invitation. Directing the congregation's eyes heavenwards symbolizes the disciples' looking up after Jesus
as he was taken to heaven. Before the eucharist/communion, a dramatic meditation may be offered, where the disciples react in words to the
sight of Christ as he is lifted up, interrupted by the two in white robes
who address them about the future coming of Christ. This dramatic presentation can lead directly into the meal together, with the drama parti-
cipants taking first and then inviting the rest of the congregation to join
them as disciples in sharing the bread and wine.*

PENTECOST

May God be with you
and also with you.
Lift up your hearts.
We lift them up to Christ.
Let us give thanks to our Redeemer.
It is right to give our thanks and praise.

With joyful hearts and thankful spirits,
we give thanks to you, Creator, Redeemer and Sustainer.
We know your presence in our own day,
but join our thanksgiving now to the eternal music of all ages,
praising you with saints in heaven and earth singing (saying):

Holy, holy, holy one, God of power and might;
heaven and earth are full of your glory.
Glory be to you, O God most high.
Blessed is one who comes in the name of the Saviour,
Hosanna in the highest!

Almighty God, in the beginning
your Spirit moved upon the face of the waters
and brought forth this earth, our home.
Your Spirit breathed life into creatures of dust
and created the mother and father of our human race.
Your Spirit sounded in the seer's sermon and the psalmist's psalm
and renewed the hearts of your people.

We give you praise, Beckoning One.
Your Spirit today is poured out upon all flesh.
Praise be to you for Jesus Christ,
crucified, risen and ascended,

and for the fulfilling of his promise
that the Comforter, the Holy Spirit,
would come.

On this day of Pentecost,
we recall your outpouring of life and power
through the Holy Spirit, burning as lively fire,
yet gentle and tender as a brooding dove.
Pour out this Spirit upon us, we pray.
Fill us with the Spirit's power,
comfort us with the Spirit's embrace,
heal us with the Spirit's touch,
inspire us with the Spirit's wisdom.

By your Spirit, our Rock and our Redeemer,
hallow this bread that we break
and this wine that we share,
that we may be caught up in your sustaining presence
as we remember Jesus' words to his disciples when he shared his
last supper with them:
'Take, eat, drink.
Do these things in remembrance of me.'
As we eat and drink in remembrance of him,
we offer our hearts in love,
our minds in devotion,
our wills in obedience,
giving thanks for Christ's love for us all.

THE LORD'S PRAYER

BREAKING THE BREAD AND SHARING THE WINE
Take, eat. This is the body of Christ given for you.
Do this in remembrance of him.
This cup is the new covenant in the blood of Christ.
Drink from it, and remember him.

THE INVITATION
Draw near to this holy table, filled with the Holy Spirit's love.

PRAYER (*following the meal*)
Spirit of the Living God, you have refreshed us with this holy mystery.
Now send us into the world to be your disciples, strengthened by your love and sustained by your courage. **Amen.**

Ideas for worship

The Pentecost prayer may be used in a celebratory setting, including decoration by banners or red cloth draped on the communion table/altar. Twelve candles can be lit prior to the Scripture reading, signifying the flames that came upon the disciples and filled them with the Spirit. Scripture verses may be read in different languages or biblical versions to signify the disciples speaking in various languages on the Day of Pentecost.

ALL SAINTS' TIDE

May God be with you
and also with you.
Lift up your hearts.
We lift them up to Christ.
Let us give thanks to our Redeemer.
It is right to give our thanks and praise.

God of yesterday, today and tomorrow,
God of our parents and children,
we bless your name.
Truly you are the dwelling-place of every generation.
In this our day and generation,
we unite our worship to the endless song of eternal ages,
praising you and singing (saying):

Holy, holy, holy one, God of power and might;
heaven and earth are full of your glory.
Glory be to you, O God most high.
Blessed is one who comes in the name of the Saviour,
Hosanna in the highest!

God of Abraham, Sarah and Hagar,
God of promise,
God of the dispossessed, we worship you.
God of Miriam and Moses,
God of faith and freedom, we worship you.
God of Deborah, Gideon, Jephthah and his daughter,
God of the remembered and the overlooked, we worship you.
God of Mary and Joseph,
through whom you brought birth to our Saviour Jesus Christ,
we worship you.

We remember Jesus Christ,
born at Bethlehem,
teaching in Galilee and Jerusalem,
crucified and risen.
We remember him breaking the bread,
sharing the cup,
and saying to his disciples,
'Do this in remembrance of me.'
We remember the apostles of the early church and the countless numbers
who have proclaimed through the centuries
the love of Christ for the world.
As you empowered the saints of old,
so may Christian peoples today
be nourished and strengthened by your presence.

Eternal God, bless this bread which we break,
this cup which we share,
the communion which we nourish in relationship with one another.
Through this offering of praise and thanksgiving,
may Christ be present in each one here.
In communion with all your saints in heaven and earth,
we offer ourselves to you as followers of Jesus Christ.

THE LORD'S PRAYER

BREAKING THE BREAD AND SHARING THE WINE
Take, eat. This is the body of Christ given for you.
Take, drink. This is the blood of Christ given for you.
Do these things in remembrance of him.

THE INVITATION
Draw near to the table where Christ meets and serves us.

PRAYER (*following the meal*)
God of all peoples, we praise your holy name.
May these gifts of bread and wine which you gave freely to us
empower us to carry forth your work in this world.
Bless us and all your saints, we pray. **Amen.**

Ideas for worship

This prayer lends itself to more than one voice, especially where some of the saints are mentioned. It has been used in a worship context where several young people and adults told stories about saints who were important to them–from biblical texts and also those they remember in their own lives. Candles may be lit for each person sharing and the person/people about whom they speak. After the time of sharing, the eucharist/communion may be celebrated as a connection to those who have gone on before.

SPRING

May God be with you
and also with you.
Lift up your hearts.
We lift them up to Christ.
Let us give thanks to our Redeemer.
It is right to give our thanks and praise.

Creator God, source of life,
we rejoice in this season of new life.
The earth belongs to you;
we who are created of the dust of the earth
offer to you the adoration of our own lives.
We praise you for the sunshine and the showers of a spring day,
we praise you for the nesting birds,
the snow melting on the hillside,
the cascading stream and rising river,
the flowers of woodland and hedgerow,
the blossom promising fruitful harvest.
We who hold all such good things in trust
give thanks to you as Good Creator,
joining in the song of eternal praise:

Holy, holy, holy one, God of power and might;
heaven and earth are full of your glory.
Glory be to you, O God most high.
Blessed is one who comes in the name of the Saviour,
Hosanna in the highest!

Source of Life, we are the children of your bearing.
We praise you for your sustenance and your love,
for spring which follows winter,

for renewal of hope which follows despair,
for every sign that shows life being stronger than death.

Especially we praise you for Jesus Christ,
who taught us that you care for the birds of the air and the lilies
of the field,
that you care for us as a father or mother caring for a child.
We praise you for the salvation which is ours
by the death and resurrection of Christ Jesus.
Enrich our communion with one another,
as we share the bread and drink from the cup by which Christ
told us to remember him.
Send your Holy Spirit upon us and upon these elements we pray,
strengthening us to be life-givers in the world.
We give our thanks to you,
offer ourselves up to you,
and bless your holy name.

THE LORD'S PRAYER

BREAKING THE BREAD AND SHARING THE WINE
On the night in which he was betrayed, Jesus said:
'Take, eat. This is my body broken for you.
Do this in remembrance of me.
Take, drink. This is the cup of the new covenant.
Drink from it and remember me.'

THE INVITATION
Draw near to the holy table in love and new life.

PRAYER (*following the meal*)
As new growth breaks through the soil,
and as blossoms burst forth from the trees,
may we be nourished by this meal together

so that we may know what it is to live new life.
Bless us as a living community, we pray. **Amen**.

Ideas for worship

This prayer may be used on any given day in spring when the eucharist/communion is included in worship. Its primary focus is to celebrate resurrection, so it is particularly appropriate at Eastertide. A spring festival celebration with flowers and plants placed throughout the sanctuary is an effective way to continue celebrating resurrection in the Easter season. After communion, children may wish to hand out flowers to the congregation during a hymn of praise, enhancing the celebration of God's creation.

May God be with you
and also with you.
Lift up your hearts.
We lift them up to Christ.
Let us give thanks to our Redeemer.
It is right to give our thanks and praise.

From the rising of the sun to its setting,
your name be praised, O Light of the World!
Truly, Jesus Christ is our sun of righteousness.
He is a sun which never sets,
he is a light which no one can extinguish.
In faith and love, we celebrate the brightness of this season
and offer to you our adoration and thanksgiving.
We join our praise with all your people in heaven and on earth,
singing (saying):

Holy, holy, holy one, God of power and might;
heaven and earth are full of your glory.
Glory be to you, O God most high.
Blessed is one who comes in the name of the Saviour,
Hosanna in the highest!

God of the summer's day, we worship you.
God of the lingering sunset and early dawn, we worship you.
God of the warm breeze and refreshing shower,
God of the growing tree and opening flower,
God of the ripening harvest and sparkling sea, we worship you.
All creation blesses the Creator, the source of energy and life.

In our praise and thanksgiving,
we remember the ways of Christ who walked the dusty roads of
Galilee,
who taught from seashore and mountainside,
who drew lessons from the sower and the seed,
the lilies of the field, and birds of the air.
May we, too, know your presence in the beauty of creation.

We also remember, Creator God,
that your care for this earth and your people can be denied;
for your goodness was abused and your son was betrayed.
On the night of his arrest, Christ shared a last supper with his disciples.
Through grain and grape, bread and wine,
Christ spoke of his coming death and new life,
asking his disciples to remember him.
Be present with us now, Merciful God, as we share this sacrament.
Let your Holy Spirit descend upon us and upon this meal.
May we feel your touch,
hear your call,
experience your grace,
know your strength in our lives.
May this bread and wine be to us the communion of our Saviour's
body and blood,
renewing us in faith and strengthening us for service.
We offer ourselves and our thanksgiving to you now through this
meal in memory of Christ's love.

THE LORD'S PRAYER

BREAKING THE BREAD AND SHARING THE WINE
Take, eat. This is the body of Christ broken for you.
Do this in remembrance of him.
Take, drink. This is the blood of Christ shed for you.
Do this in remembrance of him.

THE INVITATION
Draw near to the table, knowing God's forgiveness and healing love.

PRAYER (*following the meal*)
Generous Giver of Life, you supply us with all good things.
May this bread and wine be the nourishment we seek,
and may it transform us into disciples who serve in your creation.
Amen.

Ideas for worship

A summer celebration of the last supper can be treated like a community picnic. People gather around the table/altar and share bread informally; wine is poured into small glasses for everyone. This prayer has been used in worship both indoors and outdoors, usually with small groups. It may also be used in more formal worship.

HARVEST/AUTUMN

May God be with you
and also with you.
Lift up your hearts.
We lift them up to Christ.
Let us give thanks to our Redeemer.
It is right to give our thanks and praise.

Creator God, Source of Life,
we lift our thanks to you in this season of harvest.
The bounty of the earth belongs to you,
the fields that ripen in the sun give praise to your name.
For the colours of the autumn,
the sharpening wind,
the gathering-in of all that nourishes us,
we give you thanks.
We hold the blessings you give us in trust
and praise you, Good Provider,
for our lives, our homes,
and all that we share.
In thanksgiving, we join together in the song of eternal praise:

Holy, holy, holy one, God of power and might;
heaven and earth are full of your glory.
Glory be to you, O God most high.
Blessed is one who comes in the name of the Saviour,
Hosanna in the highest!

Gracious, Giving God, you have created us so that we may find
rest from our labours,
so that we may find space to spend time with you.

As the days shorten and our earth prepares for the sleep of
winter,
we turn to you, searching for peace.

We praise you for the presence of your Spirit
who teaches us to combine labour with rest,
who brings us the cycles of time and season,
who sustains us when we are in need.
For all the good gifts you bring us, we praise your holy name.

We turn to the table of bounty and sustenance in the name of
our Saviour.
By the death and resurrection of Jesus our Redeemer,
through the sharing of this bread and wine,
gifts of your creation,
may we be created anew.
As we hear the words in which Christ invited his disciples to take
bread and wine,
and to remember him always,
we give thanks for all that he has done for our sake.
Bless these elements, and our communion with one another.
Draw us closer to your presence, O Loving God.
Send your Holy Spirit upon us
and strengthen us in times of hardship and of plenty,
as we offer ourselves to you in thanksgiving.

THE LORD'S PRAYER

BREAKING THE BREAD AND SHARING THE WINE
This is the body of Christ given for you.
Eat in remembrance of him.
Drink from this cup of the new covenant in his blood.
As you drink from it, remember him.

THE INVITATION
Draw near to this table set before you, which brings God's
blessing and grace.

PRAYER (*following the meal*)
Source of Plenty, may our sharing become sharing with the world.
May our blessing become blessing for the world.
May our lives become living assurance of your presence in the
world. **Amen**.

Ideas for worship

*This prayer may be used as part of a Harvest or Thanksgiving Festival
in a traditional worship setting. The communion table/altar is set with
grains of wheat and red grapes in addition to the already-prepared elements. Table-setting can take place during a hymn of thanksgiving
immediately before the eucharistic prayer. It may also be appropriate for
young people to grind flour and squeeze grapes before communion, thereby
symbolizing working with the harvest to create those items needed for
communion.*

WINTER

May God be with you
and also with you.
Lift up your hearts.
We lift them up to Christ.
Let us give thanks to our Redeemer.
It is right to give our thanks and praise.

We give thanks to you, O God of mystery,
that in the darkness, you are light;
in the coldness, you are warmth.
Help us to draw nearer to you,
remembering that you offer us the strength of endurance
as we journey through the seasons of change.
May the clarity of your vision for the world strike us
as do the sights of snow-capped hills,
the frost on the fields,
the sun on a winter's day,
the clear and healing air.
As creation lies resting,
gaining strength for being born anew,
bring your hand of love upon it and bless it with health and care.
We turn our lives to you, O God, in trust and thanksgiving,
joining together in the song of unending praise:

Holy, holy, holy one, God of power and might;
heaven and earth are full of your glory.
Glory be to you, O God most high.
Blessed is one who comes in the name of the Saviour,
Hosanna in the highest!

Gentle, Quiet God, we remember the time when Jesus faced
difficult decisions and destructive forces.
He prayed that your will might be done in all life's trials.
When we too experience the dark night of the soul,
may we find the courage to let go and trust in your guiding light.
Christ has shown us that life is stronger than death;
and as we eat together at the table,
we remember the words he spoke to his companions on the eve of
his betrayal.
As he broke the bread, he told them:
'Take, eat. This is my body which is broken for you.
Do this in remembrance of me.'
Then he took the cup, gave thanks, and said to them:
'Drink from this, all of you.
This is the blood of the new covenant, poured out for you and for
many.
Do this in remembrance of me.'

Bring us new life through this holy meal.
Bless its nourishment to our bodies and your body the church.
May the Holy Spirit rest upon this bread and wine now as we
share together,
and may we as your servants be an acceptable offering in your
sight.

THE LORD'S PRAYER

BREAKING THE BREAD AND SHARING THE WINE
Take, eat. This is the body of Christ given for you.
Take, drink. This is the blood of Christ given for you.
Do these things in remembrance of him.

THE INVITATION
Draw near to the table, trusting in God's healing and renewal.

PRAYER (*following the meal*)
God of amazing grace, in the darkness of winter months, we are
grateful that you remain with us.
We give you thanks for this holy meal
and pray that it may strengthen us to follow Christ,
the everlasting light.
Bless all our days. **Amen.**

Ideas for worship

*The winter prayer may be used in a slightly darkened sanctuary, where a
single candle is brought forth with the elements. This prayer is usually
used in the month of February before Lent begins. The words are meant
to be quiet and restful, but also anticipatory of new life springing forth in
the not-too-distant future. These words are also metaphors for God's guiding light being present even in the darkest of times.*

MARRIAGE

May God be with you
and also with you.
Lift up your hearts.
We lift them up to Christ.
Let us give thanks to our Redeemer.
It is right to give our thanks and praise.

On this day of celebration, we thank you, Maker of all things good,
for the love that is found in this place.
We lift our prayer of thanksgiving to you,
remembering the words that Jesus spoke:
'Love God with all your heart and mind and soul,
and one another as yourself.'
Bring your presence to all who gather here in the name of love,
and hear us as we worship you and adore your name through our
hymn of praise:

Holy, holy, holy one, God of power and might;
heaven and earth are full of your glory.
Glory be to you, O God most high.
Blessed is one who comes in the name of the Saviour,
Hosanna in the highest!

Loving God, in the beginning of time,
you created human beings in your image.
Your hope for the earth was that we might live in harmony with
each other and all creation.
You made a covenant with all living creatures to be our God;
we wish to renew our part of the covenant to be your people.

As two people commit their lives to each other today,
we lift them to you in the knowledge that you are present in their
marriage.
We give you thanks for this gift of love
and pray that your Spirit may be present with them and with us
always.
Bring your blessing upon these two,
and on their families and friends,
that they may know your eternal presence.

On this wedding day, we recall the miracle at the wedding in
Cana where Jesus turned the water into wine.
We remember that all are invited to the wedding banquet which
you have set for us.
Pour out your Holy Spirit upon us here, we pray,
and bless the elements that are before us.
Fill us with the joy of love shared,
the peace of love felt,
and the power of love given,
as we offer ourselves to you in praise and thanksgiving.

THE LORD'S PRAYER

BREAKING THE BREAD AND SHARING THE WINE
We remember Christ's love for his disciples on the night he
shared his last supper with them. Hear his words to the disciples
again:
'Take, eat. This is my body given for you.
Do this in remembrance of me.
Take, drink. This is the cup of the new covenant in my blood.
Do this in remembrance of me.'

THE INVITATION
Draw near to the holy table now, in thanksgiving and love.

PRAYER (*following the meal*)
Loving Creator, we give you thanks for this celebration together.
In the eating of bread and drinking of wine, draw us ever closer
to you.
Bless each of us and all of us in your love. **Amen.**

Ideas for worship

The wedding prayer may be used in formal settings and also outdoors, in several denominational contexts. Included in it is a prayer of intercession for those who are marrying each other; through the eucharist/communion they are especially bound together in Christ's love through their unique relationship. Family and friends need to be invited to partake in the elements as they would have been included in the feasting at the wedding of Cana. The eucharist/communion is appropriate after the couple exchange vows and ring(s).

PRAYER OF JUSTICE

May God be with you
and also with you.
Lift up your hearts.
We lift them up to Christ.
Let us give thanks to our Redeemer.
It is right to give our thanks and praise.

We give thanks and praise to your name as Creator of heaven and
earth.
You are almighty and all-gentle,
all-wise and all-loving,
all-powerful and all-seeing;
yet in Jesus, you made a place for the powerless and dispossessed.
You are our God and the source of all being.
You are both companion and guide;
You are a God of justice.
You share our journey and challenge us to share others' burdens.
We worship you in the name of your righteousness
by joining with all your people on earth, singing (saying):

Holy, holy, holy one, God of power and might;
heaven and earth are full of your glory.
Glory be to you, O God most high.
Blessed is one who comes in the name of the Saviour,
Hosanna in the highest!

Holy God,
we lift to you all nations and races who come within the sweep of
your love.
We sin by promoting or ignoring injustice,
and you redeem us through Christ's death and resurrection.

We celebrate the blessing we know in Christ;
we embrace the call to see your vision of justice in the world.
We give you thanks that Christ is peace amidst pain,
strength amidst evil,
hope amidst despair,
faith amidst fear
and compassion amidst suffering.
Through this sacrament of bread and wine,
may we be transformed into a people seeking justice for all.

We remember Christ at the last supper,
breaking the bread and sharing the cup with those in the upper room.
We remember Christ risen from the dead,
walking on the road to Emmaus,
making himself known in the breaking of bread.
Come, voice of the oppressed,
share your love with us in this feast.
Spirit of the living God, come upon us
and upon these elements set before us,
that they may be to us the communion of Christ's body and blood,
given for all people.
Transform them into the peace and the works of your reign
as we offer ourselves to serve you
and those who suffer in this world.

THE LORD'S PRAYER

BREAKING OF BREAD AND SHARING OF WINE
Take, eat. This is the body of Christ given for you.
Do this in remembrance of him.
This cup is the new covenant in the blood of Christ.
Drink from it, and remember him.

THE INVITATION
Draw near to the table where Christ calls us to share together and
share with the world.

PRAYER (*following the meal*)
O God who lifts the oppressed,
may we find strength through this meal together.
May we use this nourishment to go forth into the world,
serving in Christ's name, with Christ's blessing. **Amen**.

Ideas for worship

*This prayer may be used on a Peace and Justice Sunday, where the con-
gregation makes a commitment to work for peace and justice in specific
ways. An idea that may be effective is to celebrate the eucharist/com-
munion and then for worship leaders to take the elements and invite the
congregation to follow them into another hall or room. This room might
contain displays and sign-up sheets for justice projects; the elements could
be placed on a special table in the middle.*

EUCHARISTIC POEM
Praise to the God of Power and Might

Praise to the God of power and might,
Praise to the God of truth and light,
Praise to the God of fire and sun,
God of the dawn and day that's done,
Praise to the God of work and leisure,
Praise to the God of joy and pleasure,
Praise to the God of wind and rain,
Praise to the God who shares our pain;
Praise to the God of tide and season,
Praise to the God of feeling and reason,
Praise to the God of wheat and vine,
Praise to the God of bread and wine.

Jesus Christ, child of earth,
Sign of our eternal worth—
'Do this to remember me,' he said.
'Drink this wine and eat this bread.
My body broken and my blood shed
For you, for many to be fed.'

Holy Spirit, gentle power,
Grace this table, bless this hour;
So we may know a deep communion,
Comfort, strength and perfect union
With Christian people everywhere,
And Christ our Saviour, Love so fair.

Creator God, we give you praise,
To you our joyful song we raise;
Our hearts in love to you we lift,
Offering talent, skill and gift;
Accept us, use us to proclaim
The glory of our Saviour's name.

THE LORD'S PRAYER

THE BREAKING OF BREAD AND SHARING OF WINE (*silently*)

THE INVITATION
Come in faith—find the joy of believing.
Come in hope—feel the joy of receiving.
Come in love—see what God gives.
Come in peace—know that Christ lives.

PRAYER (*following the meal*)
Praise to God our Creator,
Praise to Christ our Redeemer,
Praise to Spirit our Sustainer,
for all these good gifts. **Amen.**

Ideas for worship

This prayer is appropriate for any worship service, but is most effective in a small group, using several voices and possibly some quiet background music (such as music from the Taizé community). It may be used in a room where people sit in a circle and pass bread and wine to each other. Another way to pray the poem would be to have each person present speak a line, moving around the circle.

Part Two

BAPTISMAL
SERVICES

INTRODUCTION

The sacrament of baptism is a covenant that God shares with us, adopting us into the realm of the Christian Church. We in turn respond as partners in this covenant by promising our faith, love and service to God. Indeed, as we acknowledge that God's grace has already transformed us into a forgiven people through Christ's life, death and resurrection, we open ourselves to be guided by God's direction through word, sacrament and experience.

There are baptismal covenant services included here that welcome an infant as well as someone able to make his or her own profession of Christian faith. Infants will be asked later in life to renew the vows and profession of faith made on their behalf when they were young.

In baptism, Christ brings us through death to new life. We respond as we all renew our covenant with those who are professing faith for the first time. May the Holy Spirit descend upon us all as we are cleansed and born anew.

Possibilities for worship

These services have been used for several years in the Scottish reformed tradition and in the Methodist Church; they have been altered accordingly as family circumstances or needs arise. The sacrament of baptism is intended to be administered in the context of a worshipping community, most commonly at a Sunday service. This community is the body of Christ in covenant with God; therefore this setting is ideal for adopting another into covenant through baptism, while reminding those present of their own commitment to God. The church may be understood as the Christian community supporting the faith-journey of a child, young adult or adult before, during and after the sacrament takes place.

The baptismal service itself is appropriately placed after the reading of Scripture and the sermon. Entering into covenant or renewing vows of covenant is a response to God's initiating word, inviting people to become part of God's community and work. This order of service introduces God's invitation first, followed by responses from the one to be baptized (if possible), the baptismal party and supporting community.

To enhance the symbolism of baptism, it is effective to have a pitcher of water available near the font. A moment before the act of baptism takes place, the minister is invited to pour the water slowly into the font so that it can be both seen and heard. After the baptism, the minister might introduce the child, young adult or adult to the congregation as a new member of Christ's body. The congregation may respond by welcoming the new member into the church with the words included in the orders of service here. Finally, the minister is invited to give the new member or the baptismal family a flower as a symbol of new life in Christ. The family may stand with the minister(s) at the close of the service to be greeted informally by the congregation.

Note: This service uses the Trinitarian formula for baptism in inclusive language, 'God, Christ and Holy Spirit', rather than in male language, 'Father, Son and Holy Spirit'. This wording allows metaphors for the Trinity to be expanded beyond the traditional reading of Christ's command to go forth and baptize in the Trinity's name. The wording also allows discussion to ensue with families and members of the congregation about metaphors the Church uses for God and whether there are alternatives which are as meaningful. I recommend discussing these issues openly in various forums in the church as the inclusive formula is spoken in the sacrament. I have used it quite successfully in several worship and educational settings. Needless to say, the formula can be adapted as the worship leaders wish.

INFANT BAPTISM

BAPTISMAL HYMN

INTRODUCTION

Minister	Blessed be God present in this place today. Blessed be Christ Jesus who forgives us all our sins.
People	**May God's mercy and grace endure for all time.**
Minister	Through this sacrament of baptism, we are initiated into Christ's holy Church, become part of God's mighty acts of salvation, and are given new birth through water and the Spirit.
People	**We give thanks for God's gift of grace to this child (these children) and for us all.**

PRESENTATION OF THE CHILD (CHILDREN)
The parent(s) or guardian(s) come(s) forward with their child (children), and facing the congregation, says (say together):

> We (I) present our child, *Name* (our children, *Names*), to be baptized. We (I) desire that she/he/they may grow as a member (members) of Christ's body the Church.

RENUNCIATION OF SIN AND PROFESSION OF FAITH
The minister addresses the parent(s) or guardian(s):

Minister	Do you reject that which is evil?
Parent(s)/ Guardian(s)	**We (I) do.**
Minister	Do you accept the power God gives you to resist injustice?

61

Parent(s)/	
Guardian(s)	**We (I) do.**
Minister	Do you repent of your own sin?
Parent(s)/	
Guardian(s)	**We (I) do.**
Minister	Do you accept Jesus Christ as Saviour, trust in him, live according to his teachings, and promise to serve him?
Parent(s)/	
Guardian(s)	**We (I) do.**
Minister	Do you trust in the love and grace of Christ Jesus?
Parent(s)/	
Guardian(s)	**We (I) do.**
Minister	Will you nurture this child (these children) by prayer and example in the body of Christ's holy Church so that she/he/they might grow to profess her/his/their faith and lead a Christian life?
Parent(s)/	
Guardian(s)	**We (I) will.**

The minister addresses the congregation:

Minister	Do you as Christ's body reaffirm your commitment to the Church?
People	**We do.**
Minister	Do you promise to support this family before you, nurturing them in your care?
People	**We do.**
Minister	Then let us all profess our Christian faith together:

THE APOSTLES' CREED (OR CHRISTIAN CREED OF CHOICE)

THANKSGIVING OVER THE WATER

Minister	May God be with you

People	**and also with you.**
Minister	Let us give thanks to our God most high.
People	**It is right to give our thanks and praise.**
Minister	God of fire and water, in the beginning your Word created all creatures and all things. You brought forth light from darkness. You brought forth your people from slavery in Egypt, and through the ages have made covenant with them. You sent your Son Jesus Christ to us; he was baptized in the river Jordan and anointed with your Holy Spirit. Then Christ called forth his followers to share in the baptism of his death and resurrection, being born anew in the Holy Spirit. Likewise, as we are his followers, we ask that you pour out your Holy Spirit upon this gift of water and upon *Name(s)* who is (are) before us. May *Name(s)* be instilled with your righteousness, that through dying and rising with Christ, she/he/they may share in everlasting life.
People	**We lift our praise to you, O God, and to your Son, Jesus Christ, and the Holy Spirit who is present with us here. Amen.**

THE BAPTISM
The minister then takes the child from the parent(s)/guardian(s) and baptizes her/him, saying:

Minister	*Name*, I baptize you in the name of God, Christ and the Holy Spirit. The blessing of God, the Almighty, the All-gracious, the All-loving be upon you now and always.
People	**Amen.**

The minister returns the child to the parents. The baptism is repeated for each child presented. Then the minister faces the parent(s)/ guardian(s) and says:

Minister	May the blessing of Christ Jesus be with you and your child (children) and may he give you the grace to keep your promises spoken today.
People	**Amen.**

Then the parent(s)/guardian(s) face the congregation and the congregation welcomes them by saying:

People	***Name(s),* we welcome you into our church family. We accept our commitment as a congregation to encourage you and all other children in our midst to grow up in the knowledge and love of Christ. We welcome you!**
Minister	According to the promise of Christ, *Name(s)* is (are) received into the membership of the one holy, universal and apostolic Church and she/he is (they are) engaged to profess the faith of Christ crucified and risen and to be his faithful servant(s) her/his/their whole life long.

The congregation may sing a blessing after which the family (families) return to their pews. During the singing of the blessing a welcoming gift such as flowers may be given to each child.

PRAYER OF THANKSGIVING AND ENCOURAGEMENT

People	**God of nurture,** **bless all those who have gathered here in the faith that you bring life anew through living water.** **We give you thanks that your Holy Spirit moves amongst us in this place as we are reminded of our own baptism into new life.** **May we see you with fresh eyes,** **follow you with renewed love,** **and reach out to all who call your holy name.**

Encourage us to go forth from this sacramental place and spread the good news of Christ sharing eternal life with us. Amen.

HYMN

THE BLESSING

After the blessing, the baptismal family (families) remain at the church door to be greeted by members of the congregation.

INFANT BAPTISM
With both parents present and one parent committed to the Christian faith

BAPTISMAL HYMN

INTRODUCTION

Minister	Blessed be God present in this place today. Blessed be Christ Jesus who forgives us all our sins.
People	**May God's mercy and grace endure for all time.**
Minister	Through this sacrament of baptism, we are initiated into Christ's holy Church, become part of God's mighty acts of salvation, and are given new birth through water and the Spirit.
People	**We give thanks for God's gift of grace to this child (these children) and for us all.**

PRESENTATION OF THE CHILD (CHILDREN)

The parents come forward with their child (children), and facing the congregation, say together:

> We present our child, *Name* (our children, *Names*), to be baptized. We desire that she/he/they may grow as a member (members) of Christ's body the Church.

RENUNCIATION OF SIN AND PROFESSION OF FAITH

The minister addresses the Christian parent:

Minister	Do you reject that which is evil?
Parent	**I do.**

Minister	Do you accept the power God gives you to resist injustice?
Parent	**I do.**
Minister	Do you repent of your own sin?
Parent	**I do.**
Minister	Do you accept Jesus Christ as Saviour, trust in him, live according to his teachings, and promise to serve him?
Parent	**I do.**
Minister	Do you trust in the love and grace of Christ Jesus?
Parent	**I do.**
Minister	Will you nurture this child (these children) by prayer and example in the body of Christ's holy Church so that she/he/they might grow to profess her/his/their faith and lead a Christian life?
Parent	**I will.**

The minister addresses the non-Christian parent:

Minister	Do you support *spouse's name* in her/his desire to have *child's (children's) name(s)* baptized?
Parent	**I do.**
Minister	Will you encourage *child's (children's) name(s)* as she/he/they grows/grow to share in the faith, life and worship of the Church?
Parent	**I will.**

The minister addresses the congregation:

Minister	Do you as Christ's body reaffirm your commitment to the Church?
People	**We do.**
Minister	Do you promise to support this family before you, nurturing them in your care?
People	**We do.**
Minister	Then let us all profess our Christian faith together:

THE APOSTLES' CREED (OR CHRISTIAN CREED OF CHOICE)

THANKSGIVING OVER THE WATER

Minister	May God be with you
People	**and also with you.**
Minister	Let us give thanks to our God most high.
People	**It is right to give our thanks and praise.**
Minister	God of fire and water, in the beginning your Word created all creatures and all things. You brought forth light from darkness. You brought forth your people from slavery in Egypt, and through the ages have made covenant with them. You sent your Son Jesus Christ to us; he was baptized in the river Jordan and anointed with your Holy Spirit. Then Christ called forth his followers to share in the baptism of his death and resurrection, being born anew in the Holy Spirit. Likewise, as we are his followers, we ask that you pour out your Holy Spirit upon this gift of water and upon *Name(s)* who is (are) before us. May *Name(s)* be instilled with your righteousness, that through dying and rising with Christ, she/he/they may share in ever-lasting life.
People	**We lift our praise to you, O God, and to your Son, Jesus Christ, and the Holy Spirit who is present with us here. Amen.**

THE BAPTISM
The minister then takes the child from the parents and baptizes her/him, saying:

Minister	*Name*, I baptize you in the name of God, Christ and the Holy Spirit. The blessing of God, the Almighty, the All-gracious, the All-loving be upon you now and always.
People	**Amen.**

68

The minister returns the child to the parents. The baptism is repeated for each child presented. Then the minister faces the parents and says:

Minister   May the blessing of Christ Jesus be with you and your child (children) and may he give you the grace to keep your promises spoken today.

People   **Amen.**

Then the parents face the congregation and the congregation welcomes the child (children) by saying:

People   ***Name(s),* we welcome you into our church family. We accept our commitment as a congregation to encourage you and all other children in our midst to grow up in the knowledge of Christ's love. We welcome you!**

Minister   According to the promise of Christ, *Name(s)* is (are) received into the membership of the one holy, universal and apostolic Church and she/he is (they are) engaged to profess the faith of Christ crucified and risen and to be his faithful servant(s) her/his/their whole life long.

The congregation may sing a blessing after which the family (families) return to their pews. During the singing of the blessing a welcoming gift such as flowers may be given to each child.

PRAYER OF THANKSGIVING AND ENCOURAGEMENT

People   **Gracious God, in the name of your son, we pray that we might find a glimpse of you through the waters of eternal life. We give you thanks for the promise of your love for us in this place as each one is baptized. Now as we have welcomed one more (and one more . . .)**

**may we your people be the community of living
faith, transformed by your grace, now and for-
ever. Amen.**

HYMN

THE BLESSING

*After the blessing, the baptismal family (families) remain at the church
door to be greeted by members of the congregation.*

BAPTISM
For those professing the faith
for themselves

BAPTISMAL HYMN

INTRODUCTION

Minister	Blessed be God present in this place today. Blessed be Christ Jesus who forgives us all our sins.
People	**May God's mercy and grace endure for all time.**
Minister	Through this sacrament of baptism, we are initiated into Christ's holy Church, become part of God's mighty acts of salvation, and are given new birth through water and the Spirit.
All	**We give thanks for God's gift of grace to Name (Names) and for us all.**

PRESENTATION OF THE ONE (THOSE) TO BE BAPTIZED
The one (those) to be baptized comes (come) forward and faces (face) the congregation, and says (say together):

I (We) come before you to profess my (our) faith and be baptized; I (we) desire to be a member (members) of Christ's body the Church.

RENUNCIATION OF SIN AND PROFESSION OF FAITH

Minister	Do you desire to be baptized in the Christian faith?
Candidate(s)	**I (We) do.**
Minister	Do you reject that which is evil?
Candidate(s)	**I (We) do.**

71

Minister	Do you accept the power God gives you to resist injustice?
Candidate(s)	**I (We) do.**
Minister	Do you repent of your sin?
Candidate(s)	**I (We) do.**
Minister	Do you accept Jesus Christ as Saviour, trust in him, live according to his teachings, and promise to serve him?
Candidate(s)	**I (We) do.**
Minister	Do you trust in the love and grace of Christ Jesus?
Candidate(s)	**I (We) do.**

The minister addresses the congregation:

Minister	Do you as Christ's body reaffirm your commitment to the Church?
People	**We do.**
Minister	Do you promise to support *Name (Names)* before you, nurturing her/him/them in your care?
People	**We do.**
Minister	Then let us all profess our Christian faith together:

THE APOSTLES' CREED (OR OTHER CHRISTIAN CREED)

THANKSGIVING OVER THE WATER

Minister	May God be with you
People	**and also with you.**
Minister	Let us give thanks to our God most high.
People	**It is right to give our thanks and praise.**
Minister	God of fire and water, in the beginning your Word created all creatures and all things. You brought forth light from darkness. You brought forth your people from slavery in Egypt, and through the ages have made covenant with them. You sent your Son Jesus Christ to us; he was baptized in the river

Jordan and anointed with your Holy Spirit. Then Christ called forth his followers to share in the baptism of his death and resurrection, being born anew in the Holy Spirit. As *Name (Names)* professes (profess) to be a follower (followers) of Jesus Christ, pour out your Holy Spirit upon this gift of water and upon him/her/them. May *Name (Names)* be cleansed and instilled with your righteousness, that through dying and rising with Christ, she/he/they may share in everlasting life.

People **We lift our praise to you, O God, and to your Son, Jesus Christ, and to the Holy Spirit who is present with us here. Amen.**

THE BAPTISM
The minister baptizes her/him, saying:

Minister *Name*, I baptize you in the name of God, Christ and the Holy Spirit. The blessing of God, the Almighty, the All-gracious, the All-loving be upon you now and always.

People **Amen.**

The baptism is repeated for each person present. Then the minister faces the one (those) baptized and says:

Minister May the blessing of Christ Jesus be with you and may he give you the grace to keep your promises spoken today.

People **Amen.**

The one (those) baptized faces (face) the congregation and the congregation welcomes her/him/them by saying:

People	*Name (Names),* **we welcome you into our church family. We accept our commitment as a congregation to encourage you to grow in the knowledge and love of Christ. We welcome you!**
Minister	According to the promise of Christ, *Name (Names)* is (are) received into the membership of the one holy, universal and apostolic Church. She/he is (they are) engaged to profess the faith of Christ crucified and risen and to be his faithful servant(s) her/his/their whole life long.

The congregation may sing a blessing after which the one (those) baptized returns (return) to the pews. During the singing of the blessing a welcoming gift may be given to each person baptized.

PRAYER OF THANKSGIVING AND ENCOURAGEMENT

People	**Redeeming God,** **we give you thanks that we may come together as community to witness such a faith that risks death for new life.** **We give you thanks for *Name(s)* and those who support him/her (them);** **we pray that we might be connected together in our journeys from this point forward.** **Bless all who have gathered here today in celebration of your love! Amen.**

HYMN

THE BLESSING

After the blessing, the one (those) baptized may remain at the church door to be greeted by members of the congregation.

Part Three

RESPONSIVE
READINGS
AND PRAYERS

INTRODUCTION

As we have dialogue with God in worship, we experience times when raising our voices as one in praise or prayer weaves us together in our common faith. We worship both personally and as community simultaneously through the spoken word, building our relationship with God and each other.

Some of the responses that follow use imagery to bring alive the ancient setting for a liturgical day. Others speak with God about feelings that we encounter as human beings and the relationship we hope to have with God through them. Still others simply praise God's name. All the readings and prayers spring from a desire human beings have to be able to name their yearning for God's presence and to praise the blessing that God has brought to us through Christ.

Possibilities for worship

These readings and prayers have been used in a variety of congregations for calls to worship, communal praying and statements of the human condition before God. They are written for more than one voice and may be used by leaders with the congregation, by two or more people speaking for the congregation, or by individuals in the congregation speaking to each other.

Each reading may be read with dramatic impact, based on the placement of voices around the sanctuary or room. On festival days, it is effective to proclaim the responsive readings with two or three readers walking slowly forward from different points in the back of the sanctuary, meeting in the middle of the chancel area for the final three lines. One reader might remain in the back the whole time and exchange dialogue with someone in front of the congregation.

In addition to the possibilities for movement with different voices, each of these readings may be punctuated by a short musical interval before and after the reading, and sometimes in the middle. This music is helpful in setting the mood for the reading or prayer; I have found the Taizé tradition especially helpful for this. Chants or music without words played on a single instrument (such as the flute, violin, cello, trumpet for celebration days, or an appropriate setting on the organ) can be moving for the congregation listening or speaking to God through these readings and prayers.

In small groups, these prayers and readings can be used as a focus for devotional time together or as part of more informal worship. Again, several voices may be used. Leaders may move throughout the space available. Simply sitting in a circle with each person reading a line is effective as well.

The contents of the following section may also be used in conjunction with the eucharistic/communion prayers found in Part One. The seasonal outline is used consistently and lends itself to combining resources from each Part.

ADVENT

Leader	There is one crying in the wilderness who brings good news!
Side A	Come, O long-expected Messiah! Prepare the way for the Saviour!
Side B	We hear the good news ringing forth! Come and set us free!
Leader	You are Israel's strength and consolation;
Side A	you are our hope and our salvation.
Side B	How will you come to us?
Leader	There shall be born a child in Bethlehem
Side A	who shall come humbly by a mother named Mary.
Side B	And there will be a sign.
Leader	The Almighty has done great deeds:
Side A	God will scatter the proud and cast down the mighty from their thrones.
Side B	God will lift the lowly and fill the hungry with good things.
All	**We await our Saviour with joy—he shall redeem us and rule all the earth!**

CHRISTMAS

Leader   Joy to the world! Our Saviour is born!
People   **Joy to the earth! Our Saviour does reign!**

Leader   Emmanuel is with us.
People   **Christ dwells among us.**

Leader   Wisdom comes from our God most high.
People   **Light has gladdened the darkness.**

Leader   Come, all you faithful people, worship the Messiah!
People   **We gather together to behold and adore him.**

Leader   Come, all you searching people, Love has been made manifest.
People   **We raise our voices in praise and wonder.**

All   **Gloria in excelsis Deo! All praise to the newborn Christ!**

EPIPHANY

Voice 1   There is a song in the air
Voice 2   there is a star in the heavens
Voice 3   there is a lowly stable
Voice 1   there is a child to meet.

Voice 2   Let us bring our gifts
Voice 3   let us worship this child
Voice 1   let us follow the light coming from where he sleeps
Voice 2   let us seek blessing for our journey through the
          wilderness.

Voice 3   May we be held in the palm of God's hand as we meet
          our Saviour
Voice 1   may we keep the light before us.

Voice 2   May we know the gift that the Christ child gives to us.

Voice 3   May we know the love of the Messiah in our
          journeying!

LENT

Leader   Jesus was led by the Spirit for forty days
in the wilderness and tempted by the devil.

People   **We remember the forty days of the great flood;**
Noah was saved with his family
and two of every kind of living creature.

Leader   We remember the forty years of wandering in the
wilderness;
the children of Israel came out of Egypt
and looked forward to finding the land of promise.

People   **We remember Moses neither eating nor drinking**
for forty days and nights
while he received the Law at Mount Sinai
and spoke with God.

Leader   We remember Elijah travelling for forty days
towards the mountain of God
in the strength of food given to him by an angel.

People   **We remember Mary and Joseph presenting Jesus in**
the temple when he was forty days old,
a light to the Gentiles and the glory of Israel.

Leader   We remember Jesus fasting forty days and forty nights
in the wilderness
knowing the feel of earthly temptations.

People   **We remember Jesus, a man not yet forty years old,**
suffering and dying.

Leader   We remember Jesus appearing again to his followers
over forty days
before he ascended to the right hand of God.

All **Praise be to you, O God, for all your mighty acts.**
    Strengthen us in every hour of testing,
    guide us in the ways of love and truth and peace
    through our forty days of repentance
    to the time of resurrection.

PALM SUNDAY

Leader	Hosanna, loud Hosanna! The Messiah enters the gate!
People	**He comes from the Mount of Olives followed by a crowd!**

Leader	Raise your voices! Sing your praises!
People	**We will spread cloaks and palm leaves before him!**

Leader	We will wave our branches in exultation!
People	**All glory, laud and honour to you, Redeeming Christ.**

Leader	We praise your holy name in all the earth,
People	**yet we know that your passion approaches.**

Leader	Your time of suffering comes near;
People	**the shadow of the cross is looming on the hill.**

Leader	We shall not forsake you, help us not to turn from you.
People	**We shall cry 'Crucify!'**

Leader	Forgive us for what we are about to do.
People	**May we know your mercy**

All	**and the glorious victory of your resurrection to come!**

EASTER

Side A	Christ is alive! He is risen!
Side B	Christ is alive! Let us proclaim the good news to all the earth!
Side A	Love and Salvation have triumphed over death!
Side B	Neither sin nor death shall ever separate us from the love of Christ.
Side A	O death, where is your sting?
Side B	Our eyes are opened
Side A	our hearts renewed
Side B	our faith is living
Side A	our souls sanctified.
Side B	May the Church sing forth its gladness!
All	**We rejoice in our Christ always! Alleluia! Amen!**

ASCENSION

Voice A   Rise up, followers of Christ.
Voice B   Rise up, and praise our Saviour!
Voice C   Rise up, disciples of our Redeemer.
Voice D   Rise up, and give glory to God!

Voice A   For we have walked through the valley of the shadow
           of death,
Voice B   and witnessed resurrection and new life;
Voice C   for we have walked on the road to Emmaus,
Voice D   and witnessed ascension and glory!

Voice A   Come and look toward the heavens;
Voice B   come and find Christ's glory.
Voice C   Come and know that the Spirit will be with us;
Voice D   come and fill your hearts with joy,

All   For God is great and we are God's people!

PENTECOST

Voice 1   On this day of Pentecost, God sends the Holy Spirit
Voice 2   to come among us

Voice 1   as dove
Voice 2   to move us

Voice 1   as wind
Voice 2   to cleanse us

Voice 1   as fire
Voice 2   to consecrate us.

Both   **Spirit of the living God, come upon us.**

Voice 1   Fill us with your empowering strength
Voice 2   empower us with your full love;

Voice 1   send us into the world proclaiming your mighty works
in every tongue.
Voice 2   Help us be the Church that goes forth where there is
need.

Voice 1   Build us into a place that makes a haven for the
homeless.

Both   **Make us the Church of disciples filled with the
wonder of your power and love forevermore!**

ALL SAINTS' TIDE

Leader   Through the ages, saints of God have witnessed in God's name;

People   **through the ages, prophets, poets, martyrs, sages have witnessed in God's name.**

Leader   We come together in the cloud of witnesses as one communion;

People   **we raise our praises to God, the giver of life.**

Leader   We bless the earthly memories of those who now shine in God's glory

People   **and join the whole company on earth and in heaven singing unending praise.**

All   **Holy, holy, holy one, God of power and might
heaven and earth are full of your glory
Hosanna in the highest!
Blessed is one who comes in the name of the
Saviour,
Hosanna in the highest!**

SPRING

Voice 1	We give praise to God, who creates all things new,
Voice 2	who brings forth life from death;
Voice 1	who awakens our souls from sleep,
Voice 2	who brings forth new life on earth;
Voice 1	who awakens living things from their slumber.
Voice 2	We see a new heaven and earth
Voice 1	and the old passes away;
Voice 2	we know that we are restored
Voice 1	and new life shines within us.
Voice 2	As flowers burst forth
Voice 1	and lambs learn to walk and play,
Voice 2	we sing praises for the resurrection of the earth,
Voice 1	and for the cycle of seasons that embraces our lives.

All   **The Light of the World shines forth in new life! Praise be to God!**

SUMMER

Side A   Praise be to God, Creator of all things,
Side B   all praise and glory be to God.

Side A   Praise be to God for earth and sea and sky,
Side B   praise be to God for sun and moon and stars,

Side A   praise be to God for the brightness of a summer's day,
Side B   praise be to God for the mildness of the summer's
          night,

Side A   praise be to God for the sun rising in the eastern sky
Side B   praise be to God for the sunset lingering beyond the
          western isles.

Side A   Praise be to God for days of energy and labour,
Side B   praise be to God for days of rest and recreation,

Side A   praise be to God for the familiarity of home,
Side B   praise be to God for the excitement of new places.

Side A   Glory be to you, O God of creation
Side B   as it was in the beginning, is now and ever shall be,
          world without end. **Amen.**

HARVEST/AUTUMN

Leader   Let us rejoice in our God!
People   **Let the whole earth exalt God's holy name!**

Leader   Proclaim God's bounty and blessing!
People   **Proclaim God's goodness and providence!**

Leader   The yield of the earth brings us good things,
People   **the season of harvest blesses us richly.**

Leader   The grains are brought forth,
People   **the fruits are gathered together.**

Leader   The feast is set.
People   **Let all who are hungry come and eat from God's provision;**

Leader   let all who are thirsty come and drink from God's blessing.

All   **We proclaim the blessings given by our provider! We lift our offering of grateful thanks and praise in God's holy name!**

WINTER

Side A   In the darkness of long nights and the quiet of winter days
Side B   we turn to the warmth of your presence, O God.

Side A   In the season of slumber and sleep
Side B   we trust in your protection, O God.

Side A   In the time of waiting for new life
Side B   we nurture your Spirit growing inside us,

Side A   we surround ourselves with your cloak of love,
Side B   and hope for the day when we shall burst forth afresh.

Side A   May our souls be the fire keeping us alive in your word,
Side B   may our hearts be the flame that lights our way,

All   in the name of Christ Jesus, our true light. Amen.

HOPE

Side A	All our hope is in God;
Side B	hope that we find strength in our trials and companionship in our journeys.

Side A	All our hope is in Christ;
Side B	hope that we are forgiven and have no need to dwell in guilt.

Side A	All our hope is in the Spirit;
Side B	hope that we will be led on the path of righteousness to new life.

Side A	Hope brings courage
Side B	hope brings life

Side A	Hope reveals possibility
Side B	hope reveals blessing.

All	**Let us worship the God of hope together, looking toward the light of our Saviour.**

HEALING

Leader   The God of strength moves within us,
People   **the God of courage hears our distress.**

Leader   The God of hope reveals wholeness to us,
People   **the God of healing touches us when we are broken.**

Leader   When the pain overwhelms, when the burden is too heavy,
People   **we turn to our God who is comforting and strong.**

Leader   When there is brokenness, when there is unending guilt,
People   **we turn to our God who is sustaining and redeeming.**

Leader   When there is loneliness, when there is isolation,
People   **we turn to our God who is loving and ever-present.**

Leader   For God creates us, redeems us and sustains us
People   **and we are not alone. Lead us in your ways, O God, and bring us your healing touch.**

UNITY

Leader   From east and west, north and south,
           people shall come to the feast of God's reign.

People   **We come from different places.**
           We come from different perspectives;
           yet we worship together in Christ's name.

Leader   O God, forgive the divisions which demean our world.

People   **O God, forgive the divisions which disfigure your Son.**

Leader   O God, forgive the divisions which set class against class,
           race against race,
           gender against gender.

People   **O God, make us one body,**
           where there is neither slave nor free,
           Jew nor Greek,
           male nor female.

Leader   How good it is when your peoples live in unity!

People   **For in unity God's blessing is ordained;**

All   **in unity there shall be life for all!**

RENEWAL

Leader   O God who makes all things new, renew us by your power.

People   O Guide who is always faithful, lead us by your vision.

Leader   O Hope who renews all life, bring us out of despair.

People   O Friend who loves us always, challenge us to live your love.

Leader   Create in us a clean heart, O God,

People   and renew a right spirit within us.

Leader   Take from us our hearts of stone,

People   and give to us hearts of flesh.

Leader   Renew us by your Spirit all the days of our life.

People   Bring us to the place of rejoicing in the New Jerusalem of your love.

JUSTICE

Voice 1   Let justice flow down like water
Voice 2   and righteousness like an ever-flowing stream.
Voice 3   We remember all who suffer injustice:
Voice 4   prisoners of conscience and those falsely accused,

Voice 1   prisoners of discrimination, by gender, race, class or
           creed,
Voice 2   prisoners of harassment and those who suffer abuse,
Voice 3   prisoners of poverty, by the greed of the rich,
Voice 4   prisoners of malnourishment and starvation,

Voice 1   prisoners of war, by the politics of the powerful.
Voice 2   Forgive us for our share in shaping and sustaining such
           a world.
Voice 3   Jesus Christ, we tried to make you a prisoner of our
           sin.
Voice 4   Have mercy upon us and teach us to bring about
           justice and peace.

CONFESSION

Leader   O Gracious Giver of Life,
           we come before you with burdens of guilt and sin:

People   **we turn to you with repentant hearts and contrite minds,**
           asking you to forgive us.

Leader   Hear us as we confess our sins:

People   **for our selfish concerns,**
           closing other people out,

Leader   for our assumptions and prejudices,
           hurting both others and ourselves,

People   **for our fear of change and risk-taking,**

Leader   for our emphasis on differences being negative,

People   **for our deliberate acts of sabotage**
           undermining others,

Leader   for our forgetting about grace when we are called to be gracious,

People   **for our determination always to be right,**

Leader   forgive us these things, O Redeemer of Life.
           Create in us a clean heart.

All   **Renew us and set us on the path of righteousness**
         for your name's sake. Amen.

JOY

Leader	I was glad when they said to me, 'Let us go to the house of God'.
People	**With gladness and joy we worship our Creator** **today!**
Leader	Weeping may endure for a night,
People	**but joy comes in the morning.**
Leader	The ransomed of God shall come to Zion with singing;
People	**they shall obtain joy and gladness;** **sorrow and sighing shall flee away.**
Leader	Before God, even the wilderness and the dry land shall be glad, the desert shall rejoice and blossom.
People	**Before God, the mountains and hills shall break** **forth into singing** **and the trees of the field shall clap their hands.**
Leader	O sing for joy to the God of joy!
People	**God has blessed the people!**
Leader	Let us praise the name of God with joy!
People	**Let us bless God's holy name together!**

PEACE

Side A   Blessed are the peacemakers,
for they shall be called children of God.

Side B   Glory to God in the highest;
peace and goodwill upon the earth!

Side A   Help us, O Merciful Friend,
to beat our swords into ploughshares
and our spears into pruning hooks.

Side B   Help us, O Giver of Life,
to turn our tanks into tractors
and our battleships into hospitals and schools.

Side A   May we turn from laying waste the earth,
to planting seeds and fostering growth.

Side B   May we turn from hatred and violence
to reconciliation and friendship.

Side A   Let us live in peace with one another.

All   **The peace of Christ be with us all.**

CREATION

Voice 1 The earth is God's and everything that is in it.
Voice 2 From the rising to the setting sun, God's name be
         praised!

Voice 1 God of green pastures and still waters, we worship you.
Voice 2 God of earthquake, wind and fire, we worship you.

Voice 1 God of storm and calm, we worship you.
Voice 2 God of warming sun and refreshing rain, we worship
         you.

Voice 1 Forgive us for all we have threatened, polluted and
         destroyed;
Voice 2 make us better stewards who share, conserve and
         recycle as we consume.

Voice 1 Help us, Creator God, to remember that this is not our
         world, but yours,
Voice 2 and that you love it so much that you sent your Son for
         its healing and salvation.

Both   **Amen.**

SORROW

Leader   O God, hear our cry to you!
People   **We ask your presence here,**
           we ask that you incline your ear to us.

Leader   Our hearts are filled with sorrow,
           our souls are full of distress;
People   **we feel helpless in times of turmoil and loss.**

Leader   We turn to you for refuge,
           we look to you for strength.
People   **Be with us, and with all those who hurt.**
           Comfort your people;
           enable us to look toward your light.

All   **Grant us your peace, Loving Comforter,**
           and carry us in your arms in times of need. Amen.

DOUBT

Voice A   O God, we call in times of trouble,
Voice B   and cannot hear your answer.
Voice C   O God, we cry out for meaning,
Voice D   and doubt that there is anything but strife.

Voice A   Creator of all living things,
Voice B   we do not always make sense of the faith,
Voice C   and therefore begin to doubt your presence.
Voice D   We do not understand your plan for this world,

Voice A   and therefore begin to doubt that you are active in it.
Voice B   We believe;
Voice C   help our unbelief!
Voice D   For surely your presence abides with us now and
always.

All   **Turn our doubt to faith, we pray. Amen.**

A LAMENT

Leader   O God, my God, why have you forsaken me?
People   **Take this cup from me, for it is painful.**

Leader   Do not leave me in the presence of my enemies,
People   **do not leave me lost in this dark valley.**

Leader   For I am faithful
People   **and wish to walk in paths of righteousness.**

Leader   Yet I am left alone
People   **and cannot feel your guidance.**

Leader   Lead me in this time of trial
People   **and show me your light.**

Leader   Lead me to your presence
People   **and keep me safe from evil.**

Leader   Yet, not my will, but yours be done.
People   **I shall wait for my God.**

All   **Amen.**

DEDICATION OF LEADERS
Response spoken by leaders after
Words of Dedication

Voice 1   We are here this day to give ourselves to you and to
           the service of our church community,

Voice 2   we are here to be a part of the network of God's love
           which includes all people,

Voice 3   we are here to witness to the world, and seek truth,
           justice and freedom through our Saviour.

Voice 4   We ask for God's help to be faithful to the service of
           our church;

Voice 5   we ask for your support and your prayers within this
           call;

Voice 6   for we are all together ministers of Christ's gospel,

Voice 7   we are all together the children of God,

Voice 8   we are all together Christ's body in the world.

Voice 9   May we always have hearts to hear and eyes to see
           what our God would have us do and be;

Voice 10 may we stand firm in integrity and always be open to the promptings of the Holy Spirit.

Voice 11 Holy, holy, holy one, God of power and might, heaven and earth are full of your glory.

Voice 12 Glory be to you, O God most high! Hosanna in the highest!

Voice 13 Blessed are all who come in the name of our God.

Voice 14 Hosanna in the highest! **Amen.**

Celebrating Women
The New Edition
edited by Hannah Ward, Jennifer Wild and Janet Morley

The new edition of the pioneering collection of prayer and worship material by women. Three times the size of the original, it includes all the earlier contents as well as exciting new writing which reflects significant recent developments. There are prayers, litanies, hymns, meditations and poems by new writers and established figures such as Janet Morley, Kathy Galloway, Kate Compston and Nicola Slee.

All Desires Known
by Janet Morley

This classic collection of prayers has made a special contribution to the prayer life of the church. 'Inclusive' but never bland or neutral, it combines familiar forms and themes with fresh and sometimes startling imagery and language. It has become an indispensable resource both for the preparation of worship in formal and informal settings, and for private meditation.

'A highly original and stunningly beautiful anthology'
The Methodist Recorder

'A remarkable collection . . . a voice of prayer sounds here that appeals to the thought and feeling of people in our time'
Church Times

SPCK Books
can be obtained from
all good bookshops.
In case of difficulty,
or for a complete list of our books,
contact:
SPCK Mail Order
36 Steep Hill
Lincoln
LN2 1LU
(tel: 01522 527 486)